BERLIN

REMARKABLE SIGHTS

Photographed by Günter Schneider
Texts by Arnt Cobbers

JARON

The Sights of the Metropolitan City

The major sights are what determines our picture of a metropolitan city. The Statue of Liberty, Big Ben, the Eiffel Tower, the Coliseum, the Kremlin, the Forbidden City, St. Stephen's Cathedral and Brandenburg Gate – the sights symbolise the spirit that permeates a city, they give form to its name.

It is true that we pay less attention to the tourist sites when we get to know a city better. But for the visitor, they will always be the major attraction. And for anyone who wants to show the city to visitors, they are like islands of refuge which history has kindly spread around the city to make it possible to design an interesting itinerary for a visit.

Berlin has a good number of such famous sights. Some have been world-famous for a long time, others have only recently been completed or are still being built: the glass Reichstag dome, which is a new symbol of the city; Potsdamer Platz, shrouded in legend; the Federal Chancellery, the centre of power and an impressive setting for state receptions; the new "Lehrter Bahnhof", an imposing cathedral-like station of glass, which is scheduled to be officially opened in 2001.

But Berlin is also a city of lost monuments. A good number of treasures had to make way for the growth in construction in bygone ages. Much was destroyed by bombs in the Second World War. And almost as much was sacrificed in the reconstruction after the war, for example the city palace and Anhalter station. But there was also much new development, some of which has already seen its share of history, such as the Europe Centre and the television tower.

There is much to see and even more to discover in Berlin. This book aims to present the most important sights in Berlin – as a souvenir, as suggestions for trips through this rapidly changing city, as an entertaining picture book.

But a city is more than the sum of its sights. It is the people and their style, the atmosphere and the energy that make up the flair of a city. Many factors must come together to make a centre of population with millions of inhabitants into a metropolitan city. And not least, it is the speed and dynamism, the thrill of what is new and what is to come that characterises a cosmopolitan city. And these elements have never been in short supply in Berlin.

"For the foreigner who regularly came to Berlin, every new visit was a surprise. From one year to the next one had to change one's concept of the city, such was the reckless speed with which it developed both within and without ..." The writer Martin Andersen Nexö wrote these words about the time before the First World War, but they still hold true today. And the same applies to the statement by Bertolt Brecht: "There is one reason why Berlin can be preferred over other cities: because it is always changing."

There are cities that are more beautiful. There are older and larger cities – but hardly any cosmopolitan city is as exciting as Berlin. Whether we consider new architecture or the latest developments in the music, media or fashion sector – Berlin is increasingly playing a pioneer role. It is this insatiable thirst for what is new, this delight in permanent change that makes this city so unique. Berlin is inspiring, and sometimes annoying – but never boring.

Perhaps this is also because Berlin is a late developer, at least in comparison with other metropolitan cities in Europe. The first merchants only settled in the marshy Spree valley in the 12th century. Berlin grew on the right bank of the Spree and Cölln on an island in the Spree – two towns which were only combined into the "capital and residence city of Berlin" in 1701.

The double town prospered, became a member of the Hanseatic league and soon overtook its competitors. The most radical change came in the 15th century when the Electors chose Berlin as their permanent residence and built a palace on the island of the Spree. Thus, the confident merchant town became a capital city: first the capital of the Electorate of Brandenburg, then the Kingdom of Prussia, then the German Reich.

The most phenomenal rise began in the 17th century when the city rose up like a phoenix out of the ashes of the Thirty Years' War. New suburbs were developed, splendid baroque houses built, trees were planted on the later grand boulevard Unter den Linden. And as a result of the Edict of Potsdam French religious refugees, the Huguenots, came to Berlin and gave great impetus to the city.

Berlin caught up with the standard of great European architecture under King Friedrich I. Under his grandson Friedrich II., the Great, Prussia became a major power and Berlin a European metropolitan city. The state opera, St. Hedwig's Cathedral and the dome churches on Gendarmenmarkt testify to the architectural and cultural achievements of this age, which was followed by the classical period in the 19th century which is especially linked with the name of Karl Friedrich Schinkel.

In this period, Berlin grew to become the greatest business centre in Central Europe and one of the few cities with over a million inhabitants. When Greater Berlin was created in 1920 the city had 3.8 million inhabitants and was the third largest city in the world, surpassed only by London and New York. The monumental Wilhelm period was followed by the rise of Modernism: in the "Golden Twenties" Berlin was probably the most interesting city in the world for its culture.

It took the National Socialists to bring this great era to an abrupt end. Instead of the "World capital city of Germania", Berlin became a unique phenomenon in world history after 1945: divided into two halves that were hermetically sealed from each other by a concrete wall. Showcases of two bitterly conflicting state systems.

It is this heritage – the glorious and the terrible – that characterises the old and new German capital. When the Wall fell in November 1989, a new era began overnight, unheard-of urban development possibilities – and obligations – arose. The separate halves of the city needed to be joined together and the desolate centre revived. Architects from all over the world came to Berlin to design the city of the future here. The results can be clearly seen: "Europe's largest building site" has again become an urban centre. But the changes have not finished yet – Berlin is still in a state of transition.

The stone monuments of bygone eras are thus all the more important, they are unadulterated witnesses to the past glory and the forgotten misery. Perhaps they are all the more fascinating because they enable us to gain a sensation of the past that they have experienced.

This book is dedicated to them – the outstanding monuments, the less familiar attractions and the newly developed major sights of our time, which we hope will some day look back on a long and peaceful history.

Breitscheidplatz is at the heart of the "City West", the former centre of the western part of the divided city. A popular meeting place is the extraordinary world fountain by Joachim Schmettau, known as the "water dumpling". In the background is the Europe Centre with the revolving Mercedes star which is visible far and wide.

A new centre in the united Berlin: Johann Gottfried Schadow's Quadriga not only majestically rises above the Brandenburg Gate, it also rises above the new buildings on Pariser Platz. Nearby is the Reichstag building (1884–94), the seat of the German parliament which was altered from 1994–99 and now has a glass dome designed by the English architect Norman Foster.

One of the most spectacular sites in the new Berlin: The Sony Center on Potsdamer Platz with the tent-like roof over the "Forum" by the architect Helmut Jahn. On this former no-man's-land between East and West, DaimlerChrysler and Sony especially have built a whole new urban district with shops, offices, apartments, cafés, cinemas, a film museum and a musical theatre.

The new buildings on Potsdamer Platz extend as far as the Landwehr-kanal. In the front the headquarters of the Berliner Volksbank, behind it the striking tall building of the DaimlerChrysler subsidiary Debis. To the left is the state library (building 2) by Hans Scharoun (1967–78).

In the Tiergarten, the large park in the heart of Berlin, and next to the Spree is the official residence of the Federal President, Bellevue Palace. It was built in 1785 as a pleasure palace for a brother of Friedrich the Great. The offices of the Federal President have occupied the "President's egg" since 1998.

Not far from Bellevue Palace is the victory column. Those who climb it can not only enjoy a fine view of the city, they also come close to the statue "Golden Else". The monument commemorates the victorious wars fought by Prussia against Denmark (1864), Austria (1866) and France (1870/71).

Brandenburg Gate – the symbol of German and European unification. The only surviving old city gate in Berlin was mainly built in 1789, the year of the French Revolution. Like in old times, it is now again integrated into the buildings around Pariser Platz, which will soon again be a setting for embassies. The adjacent new buildings, Haus Sommer (on the left) and Haus Liebermann, are based on the pre-war buildings which were destroyed.

The new plenary chamber passed its first test when the Federal President was elected in May 1999. From 1894–1933 the neo-baroque building designed by Paul Wallot had already been the seat of the German parliament. In the 1960s it was restored as a conference centre with a simplified design, and from 1994–99 the interior was completely re-designed to plans by the English architect Norman Foster.

The Reichstag, seat of the German parliament since 1999. In February 1933 and in the last days of the Second World War fire destroyed not only a large part of the internal fittings, but also the large dome over the plenary chamber. The new dome has been open to the public since 1999; visitors can walk up a spiral ramp and literally look down on their elected members of parliament.

The Foreign Office (Auswärtiges Amt) is situated by Friedrichsgracht, an arm of the Spree in the city centre. The monumental sandstone building was built as the Reichsbank headquarters (1934–38). After 1959 it was the headquarters of the Communist SED party and the Politburo. A modern end building with a glass facade and open courtyards (1997–99) was added for the relocation of the Foreign Office to Berlin.

The Federal Minister of the Interior is the only member of the cabinet in rented accommodation – in an office building in the meander of the Spree in Moabit. A fine combination of old and new architecture arose in the 1990s on the land of the old Bolle dairy.

Until 1989, the Bonn government
maintained a "permanent repre-
sentation" (Ständige Vertretung)
in East Berlin. Now, a resourceful
publican from Bonn offers new
Berliners from the Rhine a home in
the night life of the old and new
capital under the same name. The
nights in Berlin are long because
there is no statutory closing time.

Over recent years, the splendid
old boulevard Unter den Linden
has regained much of its attraction.
The wide central strip has been
redesigned and cafés have been
established. Here we see the tables
of Café Einstein, with the Brandenburg Gate in the background.

The state opera house on Unter den Linden is the finest of the three opera houses in Berlin. It was built in 1741–43 by Georg Wenzeslaus von Knobelsdorff in the style of a temple to the Greek god Apollo. The client was Friedrich the Great, who is mentioned for posterity in the inscription over the portico.

The new guardhouse on Unter den Linden was built in 1816–18 to plans by the most famous of Berlin's architects, Karl Friedrich Schinkel. Since 1993 it has been the central memorial of the Federal Republic of Germany. In the middle of the simple room is an enlarged copy of the sculpture by Käthe Kollwitz: "Mourning mother with her dead son".

The German dome church, like the French dome church, was built towards the end of the rule of Friedrich the Great in 1780–85. The buildings form a festive framework for the Concert Hall by Schinkel and make Gendarmenmarkt the most beautiful plaza in Berlin. Since 1996 the German church has housed the exhibition "Questions to German history" (photograph above). Part of the Friedrichstadt arcades can be seen to the left of Gendarmenmarkt.

Friedrichstrasse at night. The north-south axis was heavily damaged in the war and has developed over recent years to become a district for shoppers and strollers again. The scene is characterised by numerous new buildings and the beautifully restored stucco facades of old building. This view looks south from Friedrichstrasse station.

A shopper's paradise of sparkling colour. The department store "Galeries Lafayette" is one of the most interesting new buildings in Friedrichstrasse. At the heart of the glass structure, the French architect Jean Nouvel designed two offset cones clad in plexiglas.

Karl-Marx-Allee in Friedrichshain is the most monumental street complex in Berlin. The grand neo-classical buildings of up to nine storeys extend for a distance of almost two kilometres and combine the Soviet style of the 1950s with elements from the Schinkel period.

Rich colours characterise the Quartier Schützenstrasse by the architect Rossi (with Kocher and Scheurer and the planning partners Bellmann and Böhm). On the old border strip between Mitte and Kreuzberg, a large number of new office and residential buildings have been built in recent years to plans by famous architects from all over the world.

27

Nostalgic concrete slab buildings on the bank of the Spree. Very few old buildings remain in the Nikolai district, the heart of the city of Berlin around the Nikolaikirche. For the 750th anniversary of the city in 1987 the district was rebuilt with antique forms. Downstream on the left are the Palast der Republik and Berlin Cathedral.

The Ephraim Palace was known as the "most beautiful corner in Berlin". Built in 1762–65 as a residential house for the rich Jewish banker Ephraim, it is now the southern edge of the Nikolai district. Today it is used as an auxiliary building of the Berlin city museum.

Alexanderplatz is a transport hub and the most important shopping centre for the eastern parts of the city. In the 1960s the square, which was named after the Russian Czar Alexander I., was greatly extended and surrounded with monumental "Socialist" architecture. The world clock, a popular meeting point, dates from the year of the first moon landing, 1969.

The Spree between Treptow and Friedrichshain. The "Treptowers" form an interesting office and industrial complex and a symbol of the south east of the city that is visible far and wide. In front of them is the sculpture "Molecule Man" by Jonathan Borowsky. The Oberbaum Bridge in the background, probably the finest bridge in Berlin, marks the entrance to the inner city.

The Berlin town hall, generally known as the "Red town hall" because of the colour of the bricks, is the seat of the city government and the governing mayor. This substantial fortress-like building with its 74 metre high tower has shown the self-confidence of the city since 1869.

The bank of the Spree has been rediscovered in recent years as an ideal place to live and work. The striking three-part office complex at the south-west of the inner city bears the descriptive name "Trias" and is occupied by the executive management of the German railway company. The television tower was completed in 1969, and many years later it "grew" by three metres: it is now 368 metres high.

The Hackesche Höfe in the district "Spandauer Vorstadt" have become a major element in Berlin's night life over recent years. That is not only due to the admirable renovation work, it also results from the colourful mixture of offices, small business, apartments, catering and culture. The splendid first courtyard in the Art Nouveau style has an almost Mediterranean flair on warm summer evenings.

The New Synagogue in Oranienburger Strasse shows the former importance of the Jewish community in Berlin. The synagogue itself, which was the largest in Europe when it was dedicated in 1866, was destroyed in the Second World War. The front section has been restored and contains the exhibitions of the "Centrum Judaicum". From the dome there is an outstanding view of the "Spandauer Vorstadt", the old centre of Berlin.

The Jewish Museum by Daniel
Libeskind, which was enthusiastic-
ally received by the public and
architectural critics, appears like a
broken star of David. After long
arguments about the concept of the
museum, the shining silver monolith
will now be officially opened in
September 2001. The window slits
are like scars reminding us of the
fact that Jewish culture in Berlin
and Germany was largely destroyed.

A disturbing view into the abyss of German history can be found in Niederkirchnerstrasse in Kreuzberg. This site was once the headquarters of the Gestapo and SS. The remains of the basement of the Prinz Albrecht Palace, which was destroyed in the war, now contain the "Topography of Terror".

The "Anti-fascist protection wall" surrounding West Berlin was 156 kilometres long. But witnesses to the former division have become rare in the city. The wide strip between Mitte and Wedding is the only place where part of the wall strip has been reconstructed – the Wall Memorial Site in Bernauer Strasse.

For 28 years the Berlin Wall divided the city into two halves, from 13th August 1961 to 9th November 1989. But the border, which brought death to many GDR citizens, never appeared as idyllic and colourful as here. The guard tower and section of Wall are in the Allied Museum in Dahlem which commemorates the period of division and the Four Power Status.

It was long, long ago that Brezhnev
and Honecker embraced like this.
The painting in the "East Side
Gallery", a 1.3 kilometre section of
the wall in Friedrichshain, recalls
the time of kisses of Socialist brother-
hood. Directly after the fall of the
Wall, 120 artists interpreted history
in their own way here. Today, the
paintings are listed monuments and
a tourist attraction.

In the Wall era the middle of Friedrichstrasse was the site of Checkpoint Charlie, the legendary border crossing between the American and Soviet sectors. Where the border control facilities were, there are now residential and shopping buildings. A faithful replica of the Allied control building was erected on 13th August 2000, exactly 39 years after the Berlin Wall was first built.

The art lover Friedrich Wilhelm IV. initiated the development of the museum island. At its entrance is the "Altes Museum" opened in 1830, the first public museum in Berlin. An impressive hall of columns adorns Schinkel's masterpiece which contains important works of the 19th century. The pleasure garden in front of the museum was re-designed in 1999 on the basis of old plans by Schinkel.

The empty "library" below ground level in Bebelplatz (by Micha Ullmann) is probably the most eccentric memorial site in the city. This is where students burned books by persecuted authors in May 1933. St. Hedwig's Cathedral in the background is the church of the Catholic archbishop. The state opera house is on the left. The spacious plaza, the old Forum Fridericianum, was designated by Friedrich the Great as the new centre of the city.

A unique museum complex was created up to 1930 on the island of the Spree in the heart of the city. The huge dome of the Bodemuseum, which was named after the former director of Berlin's museums, rises above the point where the two branches of the Spree meet. On the right is the Pergamon Museum. The Pergamon altar originates from Asia Minor, was built in 180–160 BC and excavated by German archaeologists in 1886. It is still the greatest public attraction on the museum island (photograph above).

Berlin does not need to hide as a cultural metropolis. The new paintings gallery in the Kulturforum, which opened in 1998, presents numerous world-famous masterpieces such as the "Man with the golden helmet" (once ascribed to Rembrandt) and Vermeer's "Man and lady drinking wine".

Hamburger Bahnhof, built in 1847, is the last surviving terminal rail station in Berlin. Since 1996 it has been a place where we can set out on an exciting tour of contemporary art. The "Museum of Contemporary Art" has major works by such artists as Andy Warhol, Joseph Beuys, Roy Lichtenstein and Keith Haring.

The Philharmonie and Chamber Music Hall are the home of the famous Berlin Philharmonic Orchestra. Because of its unusual architecture, Berlin's largest concert hall built in 1960–63 to plans by Hans Scharoun has become a famous sight. The "little sister", the Chamber Music Hall, was built to plans by Scharoun in the 1980s (front of left hand picture and photograph above).

The history of Berlin is reflected in the silhouette of the western City: the spire of the Kaiser Wilhelm Memorial Church was left as a ruin after the Second World War, and the Europe Centre with its Mercedes star symbolised West Berlin as the "shop window of the West". And the metal windsail on the Kant triangle (1995) enables the citizens of the united Berlin to see where the wind is coming from at all times.

Berlin Zoo is not only the oldest zoo in Germany and the zoo with the greatest number of species in the world. The complex situated in the middle of the city near the Memorial Church is also fascinating in its architecture. Colourful buildings, some in an oriental style, have designs to fit the animal species that they accommodate. The picture shows the elephant gate, the main entrance on Budapester Strasse.

Berlin is still a major exhibition and trading centre. The radio tower, the symbol of the fair and exhibition complex in Charlottenburg, was regarded as a technical wonder when it was opened in 1926. The International Congress Centre (ICC) built in the 1970s used a sophisticated steel bridge structure to achieve acoustic isolation of the rooms.

The Kant atrium in the Ludwig
Erhard building in Charlottenburg,
built in 1994–98 to plans by the
British architect Nicholas Grimshaw.
Below the "pulpit" in the foreground
is the trading floor of the Berlin
securities market.

The Olympic Stadium, the site of
the Olympic Games in 1936. The
stadium originally held 110,000
spectators and is the venue for
numerous major sporting events,
e.g. the annual ISTAF athletics
festival and the German football
cup final. And now that the Hertha
BSC football club is successful, it is
also used for the major German
football league.

From the outside it is a mysterious
flat metal sheet – and on the inside
a highly modern sporting arena. The
Velodrom, designed by the French
architect Dominique Perrault, is set
up to 17 metres deep into the
ground. Since 1997 it has been the
venue of the traditional Berlin Six
Day Race, the largest indoor cycle
racing event in Germany.

On the outskirts of the city in the
west is the Waldbühne open-air
theatre, built for the Olympic
Games in 1936. Every summer
concerts with major rock stars and
even the Berlin Philharmonic
Orchestra attract audiences of up to
25,000 into the spacious but
intimate amphitheatre.

The south-east Berlin district of
Köpenick became famous in 1906
when the cobbler Wilhelm Voigt
put on a uniform and claimed to
be the "Captain of Köpenick".
Now there is a bronze statue in his
honour outside the place where he
tried his ruse, the town hall of
Köpenick from which he removed
the town's cash with "his" soldiers.

It began in 1695 with a small
pleasure palace far beyond the gates
of the city. Within a few decades,
Charlottenburg Palace grew to
become a grand and impressive
palace complex which is now used
as a museum and a splendid setting
for receptions and concerts. The
extensive park is also worth a visit.

The citadel in Spandau is one of the best preserved Renaissance fortresses in Germany and the Julius Tower may even be the oldest building in Berlin. The centre of the old trading town of Spandau on the Havel has retained its small town flair with narrow alleys and old half-timbered houses.

For years it was known as the "bridge of unity" – but it was a symbol of the division of Germany: Glienicke Bridge, the famous bridge shown in spy films, which crosses the Havel on the main road from Berlin to Potsdam.

High above the water of the Havel stands the Grunewald Tower which was built in 1897 to commemorate the 100th anniversary of the birth of Emperor Wilhelm I. From the top there is a fine view of the majestic forest and lake scenery in Berlin.

Berlin is set in a region with great expanses of forest and water. The Havel widens out like a lake around Peacock Island, at the southern tip of which King Friedrich Wilhelm II. had a strange palace built: a wooden building that looks like a ruin and is painted bright white. In the south-western corner of Berlin, directly next to the Havel, is a further jewel among the residences between Berlin and Potsdam: Klein-Glienicke palace with its park containing many sculptures (photograph above).

Index of Buildings

THE PHOTOGRAPHER

Günter Schneider works as a freelance photographer specialising in architectural and aerial photography. He has an extensive picture archive and is the photographer of numerous illustrated books on Berlin. His publications in Jaron Verlag include the major photographic book "Berlin" (German, English, French), the standard work on the architecture of the new Berlin "Sprung in die Zukunft", the illustrated book "Berlin. The Living Capital" (German, English, French, Italian) and "Berlin – Aerial Views" (German, English, French).

THE AUTHOR

Dr. Arnt Cobbers is a historian and art historian, worked as a guide to the city and is currently the chief editor of the classical magazine "Crescendo". He wrote the texts for numerous books illustrated by Schneider, including the case-bound "The New Berlin" (German, English, French, Spanish, Swedish, Russian). Cobbers is also the author of the guide to Berlin's architecture from the Middle Ages to today, "Architecture in Berlin".

2nd edition 2001
© 1999, 2001 Jaron Verlag GmbH, Berlin
(Title of the original edition: "Berlin – Die Sehenswürdigkeiten" © 1999 Jaron Verlag GmbH, Berlin)
All rights reserved. This publication must not be reproduced in whole or in part without the consent of the publisher. This applies especially to reproductions, translations, micro-film and storage and processing with electronic media.
Translation: Victor Dewsbery, Berlin
Cover design: Atelier Kattner, Berlin, using photographs by Günter Schneider (front: Debis tower at Potsdamer Platz, Quadriga on Brandenburg Gate, Memorial Church with Europe Centre and Kant Triangle, Reichstag Dome; back: Brandenburg Gate and Reichstag Building)
Typography and Lithography: LVD GmbH, Berlin
Printed and bound by: Druckhaus Schütze GmbH, Halle (Saale)
ISBN 3-89773-011-1